Incredibly Easy
Seafood

Publications International, Ltd.
Favorite Brand Name Recipes at www.fbnr.com

Pictured on the front cover: Grilled Shrimp Salad with Hot Bacon Vinaigrette *(page 14)*.
Pictured on the back cover: Orange-Glazed Salmon *(page 122)*.

ISBN-13: 978-1-4127-2571-2
ISBN-10: 1-4127-2571-2

Library of Congress Control Number: 2006933324

Manufactured in China.

8 7 6 5 4 3 2 1

Microwave Cooking: Microwave ovens vary in wattage. Use the cooking times as guidelines and check for doneness before adding more time.

Preparation/Cooking Times: Preparation times are based on the approximate amount of time required to assemble the recipe before cooking, baking, chilling or serving. These times include preparation steps such as measuring, chopping and mixing. The fact that some preparations and cooking can be done simultaneously is taken into account. Preparation of optional ingredients and serving suggestions is not included.

Contents

Oven-Roasted Boston Scrod
(p. 10)

Salmon Patty Burger
(p. 24)

Tuna Noodle Casserole
(p. 16)

Grilled Fish with Buttery
Lemon Parsley (p. 18)

American Classics

Grilled Red Snapper with Tangy Citrus Sauce

Prep Time: 10 minutes • **Cook Time:** 10 minutes

¾ cup *French's® Gourmayo™* Creamy Dijon Flavored Light
    Mayonnaise, divided
2 tablespoons orange juice
2 tablespoons lime juice
1 tablespoon each grated orange and lime zest
1 tablespoon minced fresh tarragon
4 red snapper fillets, about ½-inch thick (1½ pounds)
    Salt, pepper and paprika to taste

1. Combine ½ cup mayonnaise, orange and lime juices, zests and tarragon in small bowl; set aside.

2. Season fish with salt, pepper and paprika to taste. Baste with remaining ¼ cup mayonnaise.

3. Cook on a well greased grill over medium direct heat 5 minutes per side or until fish is opaque in center, turning once. Serve with sauce.

Makes 4 servings

*Tip

Two wire cooling racks can be used for grilling fish. Generously coat racks with vegetable cooking spray. Place fish on bottom rack. Cover with second rack. Use long-handled tongs for turning and removing from grill.

New England Fish Chowder

¼ **pound bacon, diced**
1 **cup chopped onion**
½ **cup chopped celery**
2 **cups diced peeled russet potatoes**
2 **tablespoons all-purpose flour**
2 **cups water**
1 **bay leaf**
1 **teaspoon dried dill weed**
1 **teaspoon salt**
½ **teaspoon dried thyme**
½ **teaspoon black pepper**
1 **pound cod, haddock or halibut fillets, skinned, boned and cut into 1-inch pieces**
2 **cups milk or half-and-half**
   Chopped fresh parsley (optional)

1. Cook bacon in 5-quart Dutch oven over medium-high heat until crisp, stirring occasionally. Remove with slotted spoon; drain on paper towels. Add onion and celery to drippings. Cook and stir until onion is soft. Stir in potatoes; cook 1 minute. Stir in flour; cook 1 minute more.

2. Add water, bay leaf, dill weed, salt, thyme and pepper. Bring to a boil over high heat. Reduce heat to low. Cover and simmer 25 minutes or until potatoes are fork-tender. Add fish; simmer, covered, 5 minutes or until fish begins to flake when tested with fork. Remove and discard bay leaf. Add bacon to chowder. Add milk; heat through. Do not boil. Ladle into soup bowls. Garnish with parsley, if desired.   *Makes 4 to 6 servings*

Oven-Roasted Boston Scrod

½ **cup seasoned dry bread crumbs**
1 **teaspoon grated lemon peel**
1 **teaspoon paprika**
1 **teaspoon dried dill weed**
3 **tablespoons all-purpose flour**
2 **egg whites**
1 **tablespoon water**
1½ **pounds Boston scrod or orange roughy fillets, cut into 6 pieces (¼ pound each)**
2 **tablespoons butter, melted**
Tartar Sauce (recipe follows)
Lemon wedges

1. Preheat oven to 400°F. Spray 15×10-inch jelly-roll pan with nonstick cooking spray. Combine bread crumbs, lemon peel, paprika and dill weed in shallow bowl or pie plate. Place flour in resealable food storage bag. Beat egg whites and water together in another shallow bowl or pie plate.

2. Add fish, one fillet at a time, to bag. Seal bag; turn to coat fish lightly with flour. Remove fish; dip into egg white mixture, letting excess drip off. Roll fish in bread crumb mixture. Place on prepared jelly-roll pan. Repeat with remaining fish fillets. Drizzle butter evenly over fish. Bake 15 to 18 minutes or until fish flakes easily when tested with fork.

3. Meanwhile, prepare Tartar Sauce. Serve fish with lemon wedges and Tartar Sauce. *Makes 6 servings*

Tartar Sauce

½ **cup mayonnaise**
¼ **cup sweet pickle relish**
2 **teaspoons Dijon mustard**
¼ **teaspoon hot pepper sauce (optional)**

Combine all ingredients in small bowl; mix well. *Makes ⅔ cup*

Baltimore Crab Cakes

16 ounces lump crabmeat, picked over and flaked
1 cup saltine cracker crumbs, divided
2 eggs, lightly beaten
¼ cup chopped green onions
¼ cup minced fresh parsley
¼ cup mayonnaise
2 tablespoons fresh lemon juice
1 teaspoon green pepper sauce
¼ teaspoon salt
Black pepper
¼ cup vegetable oil
2 tablespoons butter
Lemon wedges

1. Combine crabmeat, ¼ cup cracker crumbs, eggs, green onions, parsley, mayonnaise, lemon juice, pepper sauce, salt and pepper to taste in medium bowl; mix well. Shape mixture into 12 cakes, using ¼ cup crab mixture for each.

2. Place remaining ¾ cup cracker crumbs in shallow bowl. Coat crab cakes with crumb mixture, lightly pressing crumbs into cakes. Place cakes on plate; cover and refrigerate 30 minutes to 1 hour.

3. Heat oil and butter in large skillet over medium heat until butter is melted. Cook crab cakes 3 to 4 minutes or until golden brown on bottoms. Turn and cook 3 minutes or until golden brown on other side and internal temperature reaches 170°F. Serve immediately with lemon wedges. *Makes 12 crab cakes*

Grilled Shrimp Salad with Hot Bacon Vinaigrette

Prep Time: 10 minutes • **Cook Time:** 5 minutes

4 strips bacon, chopped
½ cup prepared Italian or vinaigrette salad dressing
⅓ cup *French's*® Honey Dijon Mustard or *French's*® Honey Mustard
2 tablespoons water
8 cups mixed salad greens
1 cup diced yellow bell pepper
1 cup halved cherry tomatoes
½ cup pine nuts
1 pound jumbo or extra large raw shrimp, shelled with tails left on

1. Cook bacon until crisp in medium skillet. Whisk in salad dressing, mustard and water; keep warm over very low heat.

2. Place salad greens, bell pepper, tomatoes and pine nuts in large bowl; toss. Arrange on salad plates.

3. Cook shrimp in an electric grill pan or barbecue grill 3 minutes or until pink. Arrange on salads, dividing evenly. Serve with dressing.

Makes 4 servings

*Tip

To peel shrimp, remove the legs by gently pulling them off the shell. Loosen the shell with your fingers, then slide it off.

Tuna Noodle Casserole

Prep Time: 10 minutes • **Cook Time:** 11 minutes

- **1 can (10¾ ounces) condensed cream of mushroom soup**
- **1 cup milk**
- **3 cups hot cooked rotini pasta (2 cups uncooked)**
- **1 can (12½ ounces) tuna packed in water, drained and flaked**
- **1⅓ cups *French's*® French Fried Onions, divided**
- **1 package (10 ounces) frozen peas and carrots**
- **½ cup (2 ounces) shredded Cheddar or grated Parmesan cheese**

Microwave Directions

Combine soup and milk in 2-quart microwavable shallow casserole. Stir in pasta, tuna, *⅔ cup* French Fried Onions, vegetables and cheese. Cover; microwave on HIGH 10 minutes* or until heated through, stirring halfway through cooking time. Top with remaining *⅔ cup* onions. Microwave 1 minute or until onions are golden.   *Makes 6 servings*

*Or bake, covered, in 350°F oven 25 to 30 minutes.

Excellent

*Tip
Garnish with chopped pimiento and parsley sprigs, if desired.

Grilled Fish with Buttery Lemon Parsley Sauce

Nonstick cooking spray
6 tablespoons butter or margarine
3 tablespoons finely chopped fresh parsley
1 teaspoon grated lemon peel
½ teaspoon salt
½ teaspoon dried rosemary
6 fish fillets (6 ounces each), such as grouper, snapper or any lean white fish
3 medium lemons, halved

1. Coat grill grid with cooking spray. Preheat grill to medium-high heat.

2. Combine butter, parsley, lemon peel, salt and rosemary in small bowl; set aside.

3. Coat fish with cooking spray; place on grid. Grill, uncovered, 3 minutes. Turn; grill 2 to 3 minutes longer or until opaque in center.

4. To serve, squeeze juice from 1 lemon half evenly over each fillet. Top evenly with butter sauce. *Makes 6 servings*

Manhattan Clam Chowder

¼ **cup chopped bacon**
1 **cup chopped onion**
½ **cup chopped carrots**
½ **cup chopped celery**
2 **cans (14.5 ounces each) CONTADINA® Recipe Ready Diced Tomatoes, undrained**
1 **can (8 ounces) CONTADINA® Tomato Sauce**
1 **bottle (8 ounces) clam juice**
1 **large bay leaf**
½ **teaspoon chopped fresh rosemary**
⅛ **teaspoon pepper**
2 **cans (6.5 ounces each) chopped clams, undrained**

1. Sauté bacon with onion, carrots and celery in large saucepan.

2. Stir in undrained tomatoes with remaining ingredients, except clams. Heat to boiling. Reduce heat; simmer gently 15 minutes. Stir in clams and juice.

3. Heat additional 5 minutes. Remove bay leaf before serving.

Makes 6½ cups

Microwave Directions: Combine bacon, onion, carrots and celery in 2-quart microwave-safe casserole dish. Microwave on HIGH (100%) power 5 minutes. Stir in remaining ingredients, except clams. Microwave on HIGH (100%) power 5 minutes. Stir in clams and juice. Microwave on HIGH (100%) power 5 minutes. Remove bay leaf before serving.

Red Snapper, Mushroom and Black Olive Packets

10 ounces fresh small white mushrooms, halved (3½ cups)
1½ cups chopped ripe tomatoes (2 medium tomatoes)
½ cup pitted black olives (preferably Kalamata or niçoise)
¼ cup dry white wine
2 tablespoons olive oil
2 teaspoons sliced garlic (2 large cloves)
1 teaspoon dried thyme leaves, crushed
½ teaspoon salt
¼ teaspoon ground black pepper
1 pound red snapper fillets or other firm fish fillets (such as flounder)

Preheat outdoor grill or oven to 425°F. In a bowl, combine mushrooms, tomatoes, olives, wine, olive oil, garlic, thyme, salt and pepper. Cut heavy duty aluminum foil into a 12×24-inch rectangle. Place fillets in center, overlapping slightly; top with mushroom mixture. Bring longer edges of foil together and double fold to secure; double fold ends to seal, leaving room for steam to circulate inside. Grill or bake for 25 minutes. Open ends of foil packet to allow steam to escape then open the top.

Makes 4 servings

Favorite recipe from **Mushroom Council**

Lobster Tails with Tasty Butters

Hot & Spicy Butter, Scallion Butter or Chili-Mustard Butter (recipes follow)
4 fresh or thawed frozen lobster tails (5 ounces each)

1. Prepare grill for direct cooking. Prepare choice of butter mixtures.

2. Rinse lobster tails in cold water. Butterfly tails by cutting lengthwise through centers of hard top shells and meat. Cut to, but not through, bottoms of shells. Press shell halves of tails apart with fingers. Brush lobster meat with butter mixture. Place tails on grid, meat side down. Grill, uncovered, over medium-high heat 4 minutes. Turn tails meat side up. Brush with butter mixture; grill 4 to 5 minutes or until lobster meat turns opaque.

3. Heat remaining butter mixture, stirring occasionally. Serve for dipping.

Makes 4 servings

Tasty Butters

Hot & Spicy Butter
   ⅓ **cup butter, melted**
   1 tablespoon chopped onion
   2 to 3 teaspoons hot pepper sauce
   1 teaspoon dried thyme
   ¼ **teaspoon ground allspice**

Scallion Butter
   ⅓ **cup butter, melted**
   1 tablespoon finely chopped green onion tops
   1 tablespoon lemon juice
   1 teaspoon grated lemon peel
   ¼ **teaspoon black pepper**

Chili-Mustard Butter
   ⅓ **cup butter, melted**
   1 tablespoon chopped onion
   1 tablespoon Dijon mustard
   1 teaspoon chili powder

For each butter sauce, combine ingredients in small bowl.

Salmon Patty Burgers

1 can (about 14 ounces) red salmon, drained and bones removed
1 egg white
2 tablespoons toasted wheat germ
1 tablespoon dried onion flakes
1 tablespoon capers, drained
½ teaspoon dried thyme
¼ teaspoon black pepper
Nonstick cooking spray
4 whole wheat buns, split
2 tablespoons Dijon mustard
4 tomato slices
4 thin slices red onion *or* 8 dill pickle slices
4 lettuce leaves

1. Place salmon in medium bowl; mash skin with fork and flake salmon. (If you prefer, discard skin.) Add egg white, wheat germ, onion flakes, capers, thyme and pepper; mix well.

2. Divide into 4 portions and shape into firm patties. Place on plate; cover with plastic wrap and refrigerate 1 hour or until firm.

3. Spray large skillet with cooking spray. Cook patties on medium heat 5 minutes per side.

4. Spread cut sides of buns lightly with mustard. Place patties on bottoms of buns; top with tomato and onion slices, lettuce leaves and tops of buns.

Makes 4 servings

*Tip

Red salmon is more expensive with a firm texture and deep red color. Pink salmon is less expensive with a light pink color. While both varieties will work well in this recipe, the higher fat content of red salmon will result in slightly juicier burgers.

Pineapple-Ginger Shrimp Cocktail

9 fresh pineapple spears (about 1 package), divided
¼ cup apricot preserves
1 tablespoon finely chopped onion
½ teaspoon grated fresh ginger
⅛ teaspoon black pepper
½ pound cooked medium shrimp (about 30)
1 medium red or green bell pepper, cored and cut into 12 strips

1. Chop 3 pineapple spears into bite-size pieces; combine with preserves, onion, ginger and black pepper in medium bowl.

2. Evenly arrange shrimp, bell pepper strips and remaining pineapple spears on 6 individual plates or in 6 cocktail glasses. Top with pineapple mixture. *Makes 6 servings*

Lobster Roll

1 pound cooked lobster meat
¾ cup plain lowfat STONYFIELD FARM® Yogurt
¼ cup mayonnaise
1 cup celery, diced small
¾ teaspoon chopped fresh tarragon
6 top-split hot dog rolls
Salt & pepper to taste

Cut the lobster meat into ½-inch pieces and place them in a mixing bowl. Add the yogurt, mayonnaise, celery and tarragon. Toss well. Toast hot dog rolls. Using a spoon, gently place the chunks of lobster in the rolls and serve immediately. Be sure to refrigerate any remaining lobster filling. *Makes 6 servings*

Seafood Newburg Casserole

1 can (10¾ ounces) condensed cream of shrimp soup, undiluted
½ cup half-and-half
1 tablespoon dry sherry
¼ teaspoon ground red pepper
3 cups cooked rice
2 cans (6 ounces each) lump crabmeat, drained and picked over
¼ pound medium raw shrimp, peeled and deveined
¼ pound raw bay scallops
1 jar (4 ounces) pimientos, drained and chopped
¼ cup finely chopped fresh parsley

1. Preheat oven to 350°F. Spray 2½-quart casserole with nonstick cooking spray.

2. Whisk together soup, half-and-half, sherry and red pepper in large bowl until blended. Add rice, crabmeat, shrimp, scallops and pimientos; toss well.

3. Transfer mixture to prepared casserole. Cover; bake 25 minutes or until shrimp and scallops are opaque. Sprinkle with parsley before serving.

Makes 6 servings

*Tip

When purchasing scallops, select those with a creamy white color, a shiny texture and a sweet smell. Scallops that appear to be stark white have been soaked in water and might not be the best buy for your money. Scallops should be used within one day of purchase to guarantee freshness.

Chesapeake Crab Strata

¼ cup (½ stick) butter or margarine, melted
4 cups unseasoned croutons
2 cups (8 ounces) shredded Cheddar cheese
2 cups milk
8 eggs, beaten
½ teaspoon dry mustard
½ teaspoon seafood seasoning
    Salt and black pepper
1 pound crabmeat, picked over and flaked

1. Preheat oven to 325°F. Pour butter into 11×7-inch baking dish. Spread croutons over melted butter. Top with cheese; set aside.

2. Combine milk, eggs, mustard, seafood seasoning, salt and pepper; mix well. Pour egg mixture over cheese in dish; sprinkle with crabmeat. Bake 50 minutes or until mixture is set. Remove from oven and let stand about 10 minutes before serving.   *Makes 6 to 8 servings*

Wasabi Crab Roll

2 cans (6 ounces each) lump crab meat,* drained and picked over
½ cup *French's® Gourmayo™* Wasabi Horseradish Light Mayonnaise
¼ cup *French's®* Spicy Brown Mustard
½ cup finely chopped celery
2 tablespoons pickle relish
4 soft hoagie or hot dog rolls, split and toasted
    Lettuce leaves (optional)

Tip: You may substitute 1½ cups flaked imitation crab or chopped, cooked shrimp.

1. Mix crab, mayonnaise, mustard, celery and relish in large bowl until well blended.

2. Spoon mixture into lettuce-lined rolls.   *Makes 4 servings*

Creamy Slow Cooker Seafood Chowder

1 quart (4 cups) half-and-half
2 cans (14½ ounces each) whole white potatoes, drained and cubed
2 cans (10¾ ounces) condensed cream of mushroom soup, undiluted
1 bag (16 ounces) frozen hash brown potatoes, thawed
1 medium onion, minced
½ cup (1 stick) butter, cut in small pieces
1 teaspoon salt
1 teaspoon black pepper
5 cans (about 8 ounces each) whole oysters, drained and rinsed
2 cans (about 6 ounces each) minced clams
2 cans (about 4 ounces each) cocktail shrimp, drained and rinsed

Slow Cooker Directions

1. Combine half-and-half, canned potatoes, soup, hash brown potatoes, onion, butter, salt and pepper in 5- or 6-quart slow cooker. Mix well.

2. Add oysters, clams and shrimp; stir gently.

3. Cover; cook on LOW 4 to 5 hours.   *Makes 8 to 10 servings*

Grilled Salmon Niçoise

Prep Time: 10 minutes • **Cook Time:** 5 minutes

½ cup *French's® Gourmayo™* **Wasabi Horseradish Light Mayonnaise**
⅓ **cup plain nonfat yogurt**
1 **tablespoon minced fresh dill weed**
4 **pieces salmon fillet (about 1½ pounds total), each about 4×2×1-inches**
  Salt and pepper
1 **large head Boston or red leaf lettuce, washed and torn**
2 **cups cauliflower florets, blanched**
1 **cup sugar snap peas**
1 **bunch radishes, washed, trimmed and quartered**
½ **cup pitted oil cured olives**

1. Combine mayonnaise, yogurt and dill in small bowl; set aside.

2. Season salmon with salt and pepper to taste. Cook on preheated, greased electric grill pan or barbecue grill 5 minutes or until fish is opaque in center.

3. Arrange remaining ingredients on platter. Place fish fillets on top. Serve with dressing.   *Makes 4 servings*

*Tip

To blanch vegetables, cook 1 to 2 minutes in boiling water. Immediately drain and rinse with cold water or chill in ice water, then drain.

Simple Summer Pasta Salad
(p. 60)

Easy Calzones
(p. 42)

Orzo Pasta with Shrimp
(p. 48)

Frutti di Mare
(p. 58)

Italian Cuisine

Red Clam Sauce with Vegetables

2 cups sliced fresh mushrooms
1 can (14½ ounces) no-salt-added stewed tomatoes, undrained
1 cup chopped green bell pepper
1 can (8 ounces) no-salt-added tomato sauce
½ cup chopped onion
1½ teaspoons dried basil
¾ teaspoon dried savory leaves
½ teaspoon black pepper
1 small yellow squash, halved and sliced
2 cans (6½ ounces each) minced clams, drained and liquid reserved
2 tablespoons cornstarch
3 cups hot cooked spaghetti

1. Combine mushrooms, tomatoes with juice, bell pepper, tomato sauce, onion, basil, savory and black pepper in large saucepan. Bring to a boil over medium-high heat. Reduce heat to medium. Cover and cook 5 to 6 minutes or until vegetables are tender.

2. Stir in squash and clams. Combine ½ cup clam liquid and cornstarch in small bowl. Stir into mixture in saucepan. Cook and stir over medium heat until mixture boils and thickens. Cook and stir 2 minutes more. Serve over spaghetti. *Makes 4 servings*

Seafood Pasta

½ cup olive oil
1 pound asparagus, cut into 1-inch pieces
1 cup chopped green onions
5 teaspoons chopped garlic
1 package (about 16 ounces) linguine, cooked and drained
1 pound medium shrimp, peeled, deveined and cooked
1 package (8 ounces) imitation crabmeat
1 package (8 ounces) imitation lobster
1 can (8 ounces) sliced black olives, drained

1. Preheat oven to 350°F. Spray 4-quart casserole with nonstick cooking spray. Heat oil in large skillet over medium heat. Add asparagus, green onions and garlic; cook and stir until tender.

2. Combine asparagus mixture, linguine, seafood and olives in prepared casserole. Bake 30 minutes or until heated through.   *Makes 6 servings*

Italian Fish Soup

1 fresh halibut or haddock steak (about 4 ounces)
1 cup meatless pasta sauce
¾ cup fat-free reduced-sodium chicken broth
1 teaspoon dried Italian seasoning
¾ cup uncooked small pasta shells
1½ cups frozen vegetable blend, such as broccoli, carrots and water chestnuts or broccoli, carrots and cauliflower

1. Remove skin from fish. Cut fish into 1-inch pieces. Cover and refrigerate until needed.

2. Combine pasta sauce, broth, ¾ cup water and Italian seasoning in medium saucepan. Bring to a boil. Stir in pasta. Return to a boil. Reduce heat and simmer, covered, 5 minutes.

3. Stir in fish and frozen vegetables. Return to a boil. Reduce heat and simmer, covered, 4 to 5 minutes or until fish flakes easily when tested with fork and pasta is tender.   *Makes 2 servings*

Easy
Calzones

Prep Time: 25 minutes

1 can (10 ounces) refrigerated ready-to-use pizza dough
1 package (10 ounces) frozen chopped spinach, thawed
1 (7-ounce) STARKIST Flavor Fresh Pouch® Tuna (Albacore or Chunk Light)
1 cup chopped tomatoes
2 cans (4 ounces each) sliced mushrooms, drained
1 cup shredded low-fat Cheddar or mozzarella cheese
1 teaspoon Italian seasoning or dried oregano
1 teaspoon dried basil
¼ teaspoon garlic powder
   Vegetable oil
   Cornmeal (optional)
1 can (8 ounces) pizza sauce

Preheat oven to 425°F. Unroll pizza dough onto a lightly floured board; cut crosswise into 2 equal pieces. Roll each piece of dough into a 12-inch circle.

Squeeze all liquid from spinach; chop fine. Over the bottom half of each circle of dough, sprinkle spinach, tuna, tomatoes, mushrooms, cheese and seasonings to within 1 inch of bottom edge. Fold top half of dough over filling, leaving bottom edge uncovered. Moisten bottom edge of dough with a little water, then fold bottom edge of dough over top edge, sealing with fingers or crimping with fork. Brush top of dough lightly with oil; sprinkle with cornmeal if desired. Place 2 filled calzones on ungreased baking sheet; bake for 25 to 30 minutes, or until deep golden brown.

Meanwhile, in saucepan, heat pizza sauce. Cut each calzone in half crosswise to serve. Pass sauce to spoon over.   *Makes 4 servings*

Seafood Lasagna

1 package (16 ounces) lasagna noodles
2 tablespoons butter or margarine
1 large onion, finely chopped
1 package (8 ounces) cream cheese, cut into ½-inch pieces, softened
1½ cups small curd cottage cheese
2 teaspoons dried basil
½ teaspoon salt
⅛ teaspoon black pepper
1 egg, lightly beaten
2 cans (10¾ ounces each) condensed cream of mushroom soup, undiluted
⅓ cup milk
1 clove garlic, minced
½ pound bay scallops, rinsed and patted dry
½ pound flounder fillets, rinsed, patted dry and cut into ½-inch cubes
½ pound medium raw shrimp, peeled and deveined
½ cup dry white wine
1 cup (4 ounces) shredded mozzarella cheese
2 tablespoons grated Parmesan cheese

1. Cook lasagna noodles according to package directions; drain.

2. Melt butter in large skillet over medium heat. Cook onion until tender, stirring frequently. Stir in cream cheese, cottage cheese, basil, salt and pepper; mix well. Stir in egg; set aside.

3. Combine soup, milk and garlic in large bowl until well blended. Stir in scallops, fish fillets, shrimp and wine.

4. Preheat oven to 350°F. Grease 13×9-inch baking pan. Place layer of noodles in prepared pan, overlapping noodles. Spread half the cheese mixture over noodles. Place layer of noodles over cheese mixture and top with half of seafood mixture. Repeat layers. Sprinkle with mozzarella and Parmesan cheeses.

5. Bake 45 minutes or until bubbly. Let stand 10 minutes before cutting.
Makes 8 to 10 servings

Foolproof Clam
Fettuccine

1 package (6 ounces) fettuccine-style noodles with creamy cheese sauce mix
¾ cup milk
1 can (6½ ounces) chopped clams, undrained
¼ cup (1 ounce) grated Parmesan cheese
1 teaspoon parsley flakes
1 can (4 ounces) mushroom stems and pieces, drained
2 tablespoons diced pimiento
1⅓ cups *French's*® French Fried Onions, divided

Preheat oven to 375°F. In large saucepan, cook noodles according to package directions; drain. Return hot noodles to saucepan; stir in sauce mix, milk, undrained clams, Parmesan cheese, parsley flakes, mushrooms, pimiento and ⅔ *cup* French Fried Onions. Heat and stir 3 minutes or until bubbly. Pour into 10×6-inch baking dish. Bake, covered, at 375°F for 30 minutes or until thickened. Place remaining ⅔ *cup* onions around edges of casserole; bake, uncovered, 3 minutes or until onions are golden brown.   *Makes 4 servings*

Microwave Directions: Prepare noodle mixture as above; pour into 10×6-inch microwave-safe dish. Cook, covered, on HIGH 4 to 6 minutes or until heated through. Stir noodle mixture halfway through cooking time. Top with remaining onions as above; cook, uncovered, 1 minute. Let stand 5 minutes.

Sicilian Fish and Rice Bake

Prep Time: 6 minutes • **Cook Time:** 58 minutes • **Stand Time:** 5 minutes

   3 tablespoons olive or vegetable oil
   ¾ cup chopped onion
   ½ cup chopped celery
   1 clove garlic, minced
   ½ cup uncooked long-grain white rice
   2 cans (14.5 ounces each) CONTADINA® Recipe Ready Diced
       Tomatoes, undrained
   1 teaspoon salt
   1 teaspoon ground black pepper
   ½ teaspoon granulated sugar
   ⅛ teaspoon cayenne pepper
   1 pound firm white fish
   ¼ cup finely chopped fresh parsley

1. Heat oil in large skillet. Add onion, celery and garlic; sauté for 2 to 3 minutes or until vegetables are tender.

2. Stir in rice; sauté for 5 minutes or until rice browns slightly. Add undrained tomatoes, salt, black pepper, sugar and cayenne pepper; mix well.

3. Place fish in bottom of greased 12×7½-inch baking dish. Spoon rice mixture over fish; cover with foil.

4. Bake in preheated 400°F oven for 45 to 50 minutes or until rice is tender. Let stand for 5 minutes before serving. Sprinkle with parsley.

Makes 6 servings

Orzo Pasta with Shrimp

8 ounces uncooked orzo pasta
3 tablespoons plus ½ teaspoon FILIPPO BERIO® Olive Oil, divided
3 cloves garlic, minced
1¼ pounds raw small shrimp, shelled and deveined
1½ medium tomatoes, chopped
2 tablespoons chopped fresh cilantro
2 tablespoons chopped fresh Italian parsley
Juice of 1 lemon
2 ounces feta cheese, crumbled
Salt and freshly ground black pepper

Cook pasta according to package directions until al dente (tender but still firm). Drain. Toss with ½ teaspoon olive oil; set aside. Heat remaining 3 tablespoons olive oil in large skillet over medium heat until hot. Add garlic; cook and stir 2 to 3 minutes or until golden. Add shrimp; cook and stir 3 to 5 minutes or until shrimp are opaque. *(Do not overcook.)* Stir in pasta. Add tomatoes, cilantro, parsley and lemon juice. Sprinkle with feta cheese. Season to taste with salt and pepper.   *Makes 4 servings*

*Tip

The word orzo actually means barley, even though the shape of this pasta looks more like rice. It is available in the pasta sections of large supermarkets.

Primavera Sauce with Artichoke and Shrimp

Prep Time: 12 minutes • **Cook Time:** 12 minutes

2 tablespoons olive oil
1 cup diced carrots
1 cup diced celery
1 small onion, diced
3 cloves garlic, finely chopped
1 can (28 ounces) CONTADINA® Recipe Ready Crushed Tomatoes with Italian Herbs
½ teaspoon salt
¼ teaspoon ground black pepper
8 ounces medium raw shrimp, peeled and deveined
1 cup sliced artichoke hearts, drained
Fresh chopped basil (optional)

1. Heat oil in large skillet over high heat. Add carrots, celery, onion and garlic. Cook for 4 to 5 minutes or until carrots are crisp-tender.

2. Add crushed tomatoes, salt and pepper. Bring to boil. Add shrimp and artichoke hearts. Cook for 2 to 3 minutes or until shrimp turn pink.

3. Reduce heat to low; simmer for 2 minutes to blend flavors. Sprinkle with basil. Serve over hot cooked pasta or rice, if desired.

Makes 6 servings

Angel Hair Pasta with Seafood Sauce

½ pound firm whitefish, such as sea bass, monkfish or grouper
2 teaspoons olive oil
½ cup chopped onion
2 cloves garlic, minced
3 pounds fresh plum tomatoes, seeded and chopped
¼ cup chopped fresh basil
2 tablespoons chopped fresh oregano
1 teaspoon red pepper flakes
½ teaspoon sugar
2 bay leaves
½ pound fresh bay scallops or shucked oysters
8 ounces uncooked angel hair pasta
2 tablespoons chopped fresh parsley

1. Cut whitefish into ¾-inch pieces. Set aside.

2. Heat oil in large nonstick skillet over medium heat; add onion and garlic. Cook and stir 3 minutes or until onion is tender. Reduce heat to low; add tomatoes, basil, oregano, red pepper flakes, sugar and bay leaves. Cook, uncovered, 15 minutes, stirring occasionally.

3. Add whitefish and scallops. Cook, uncovered, 3 to 4 minutes or until fish flakes easily when tested with fork and scallops are opaque. Remove and discard bay leaves. Set sauce aside.

4. Cook pasta according to package directions, omitting salt. Drain well.

5. Combine pasta with seafood sauce in large serving bowl; mix well. Sprinkle with parsley. Serve immediately. *Makes 6 servings*

Red Snapper Scampi

Prep and Cook Time: 12 minutes

¼ cup (½ stick) butter or margarine, softened
1 tablespoon white wine
1½ teaspoons minced garlic
½ teaspoon grated lemon peel
⅛ teaspoon black pepper
1½ pounds red snapper, orange roughy or grouper fillets
(about 4 to 5 ounces each)

1. Preheat oven to 450°F. Combine butter, wine, garlic, lemon peel and pepper in small bowl; stir to blend.

2. Place fish on foil-lined shallow baking pan. Top with seasoned butter. Bake 10 to 12 minutes or until fish flakes easily when tested with fork.

Makes 4 servings

*Tip

Serve fish over mixed salad greens or hot cooked rice, if desired. Or, add sliced carrots, zucchini and bell pepper cut into matchstick-size strips to the fish in the baking pan for an easy vegetable side dish.

Scallops with Linguine and Spinach

2 to 3 tablespoons olive oil
1½ cups finely chopped onion
1 cup slivered red bell pepper
2 tablespoons minced garlic
⅛ to ¼ teaspoon ground red pepper
⅓ cup fresh lemon juice
1 tablespoon packed brown sugar
1 tablespoon minced lemon peel
1 teaspoon salt
1 teaspoon black pepper
¾ pound cooked linguine
1 (10-ounce) package frozen, chopped spinach, thawed and drained
1½ pounds cooked scallops
⅓ cup feta cheese, coarsely crumbled

Heat oil in large heavy skillet over medium-low heat. Add onion, bell pepper, garlic and ground red pepper; cook, uncovered, until tender, about 10 minutes. Add lemon juice, brown sugar, lemon peel, salt and pepper; cook 1 minute.

While preparing onion mixture, cook pasta until tender, 8 to 10 minutes. About one minute before pasta is done, add spinach. Drain pasta and spinach and place in large, warm serving bowl. Add onion mixture and toss to coat. Taste and adjust seasonings. Add cooked and warmed scallops to pasta and sprinkle with feta cheese. *Makes 4 servings*

Favorite recipe from **National Fisheries Institute**

Shrimp Fettuccine

Prep and Cook Time: 20 minutes

4 ounces egg or spinach fettucine
½ pound medium raw shrimp, peeled and deveined
1 clove garlic, minced
1 tablespoon olive oil
1 can (14½ ounces) DEL MONTE® Diced Tomatoes with Basil, Garlic & Oregano
½ cup whipping cream
¼ cup sliced green onions

1. Cook pasta according to package directions; drain.

2. Cook shrimp and garlic in large skillet in oil over medium-high heat until shrimp are pink and opaque.

3. Stir in undrained tomatoes; simmer 5 minutes. Blend in cream and green onions; heat through. *Do not boil.* Serve over hot pasta.

Makes 3 to 4 servings

*Tip

Shrimp are grouped for retail purposes by their size. The most common sizes are jumbo (11 to 15 per pound), large (21 to 30), medium (31 to 35) and small (36 to 45).

Frutti di Mare

Prep Time: 20 minutes • **Cook Time:** 35 minutes

¼ **cup olive oil**
6 **large mushrooms, chopped (about 4 ounces)**
1 **large onion, chopped**
2 **cloves garlic, finely chopped**
1 **jar (1 pound 10 ounces) RAGÚ® ROBUSTO!® Pasta Sauce**
½ **cup chicken broth**
⅓ **cup lemon juice**
1 **dozen littleneck clams, well scrubbed**
1 **dozen mussels, beards removed and well scrubbed**
1 **lobster (about 1¼ pounds), cut into 2-inch pieces**
1 **pound bay scallops**
1 **box (16 ounces) spaghetti, cooked and drained**

In large saucepan, heat olive oil over medium-high heat and cook mushrooms, onion and garlic, stirring occasionally, 5 minutes or until tender. Stir in Pasta Sauce, chicken broth and lemon juice. Bring to a boil over high heat.

Reduce heat and simmer covered, stirring occasionally, 20 minutes. Add clams and mussels and simmer covered 5 minutes or until shells open. Remove shellfish as they open. (Discard any unopened clams or mussels.) Add lobster and scallops and simmer 3 minutes or until done. To serve, arrange shellfish over hot spaghetti and top with Sauce. Sprinkle, if desired, with chopped parsley. *Makes 8 servings*

Simple Summer Pasta Salad

8 ounces uncooked bow tie pasta
2 large ripe tomatoes, seeded and chopped
1 package (8 ounces) fresh mozzarella cheese, cut into ½-inch pieces
1 can (6 ounces) tuna packed in water, drained
⅓ cup coarsely chopped fresh basil
1 clove garlic, minced
¾ cup Italian salad dressing
Black pepper

1. Cook pasta according to package directions; drain.

2. Combine tomatoes, mozzarella, tuna, basil and garlic in large bowl; toss gently. Add pasta and salad dressing; toss lightly to coat. Season with pepper to taste. Refrigerate before serving. *Makes 6 to 8 servings*

Skillet Shrimp Scampi

Prep Time: 5 minutes • **Cook Time:** 3 to 5 minutes

2 teaspoons BERTOLLI® Olive Oil
2 pounds uncooked shrimp, peeled and deveined
⅔ cup LAWRY'S® Herb & Garlic Marinade
¼ cup finely chopped green onion, including tops

In large nonstick skillet, heat oil over medium heat. Add shrimp and Herb & Garlic Marinade. Cook, stirring often, until shrimp turn pink, about 3 to 5 minutes. Stir in green onions. *Makes 4 to 6 servings*

Meal Idea: Serve over hot, cooked rice, orzo or your favorite pasta.

Serving Suggestions: This dish is wonderful served chilled with toothpicks as an appetizer. Try serving chilled then tossed in a pasta or green salad. Take it to your next picnic! Also delicious using LAWRY'S® Lemon Pepper Marinade.

**Salmon with Cranberry-
Poblano Salsa (p. 82)**

**Garlic Shrimp Burritos
(p. 96)**

Spicy Fish Tacos
with Fresh Salsa (p. 94)

Fillets with Mole Verde
(p. 76)

South of the Border

Easy
Paella

Prep Time: 30 minutes

1 medium onion, chopped
1 large red or green bell pepper, sliced
1 clove garlic, minced
2 tablespoons vegetable oil
1 can (16 ounces) tomatoes with juice, cut up
1 package (9 ounces) frozen artichoke hearts, cut into quarters
½ cup dry white wine
½ teaspoon dried thyme
¼ teaspoon salt
⅛ teaspoon saffron or turmeric
2 cups cooked rice
1 cup frozen peas
½ pound large shrimp, peeled and deveined
1 (3-ounce) STARKIST Flavor Fresh Pouch® Tuna (Albacore or Chunk Light)

In a large skillet, sauté onion, bell pepper and garlic in oil for 3 minutes. Stir in tomatoes with juice, artichoke hearts, wine and seasonings. Bring to a boil; reduce heat. Simmer for 10 minutes. Stir in rice, peas, shrimp and tuna. Cook for 3 to 5 minutes more or until shrimp turn pink and mixture is heated.

Makes 4 servings

Fish Taco Salad

2 cups shredded romaine hearts
1 medium cucumber (about 8 inches), seeded and chopped
⅔ cup cherry or grape tomatoes, halved and seeded
½ cup chopped celery
¾ cup (about 6 ounces) cooked cod or other firm white fish, flaked
Juice of ½ lime
1 tablespoon olive oil
¼ teaspoon black pepper
¼ cup sour cream
¼ cup salsa
1 teaspoon sugar
11 to 15 baked corn tortilla chips (about 1 ounce)

1. Combine romaine, cucumber, tomatoes, celery and fish in large bowl.

2. Whisk together lime juice, olive oil and black pepper in small bowl. Pour dressing over salad and toss lightly. Divide salad evenly between 2 serving plates.

3. Whisk together sour cream, salsa and sugar in small bowl. Pour evenly down center of each salad. Crumble tortilla chips down each side of sour cream mixture.   *Makes 2 servings*

Grilled Salmon Quesadillas with Cucumber Salsa

Prep and Cook Time: 20 minutes

1 medium cucumber, peeled, seeded and finely chopped
½ cup green or red salsa
1 (8-ounce) salmon fillet
3 tablespoons olive oil, divided
4 (10-inch) flour tortillas, warmed
6 ounces goat cheese, crumbled *or* 1½ cups (6 ounces)
    shredded Monterey Jack cheese
¼ cup drained sliced pickled jalapeño peppers

1. Prepare grill for direct cooking. Combine cucumber and salsa in small bowl; set aside.

2. Brush salmon with 2 tablespoons oil. Grill, covered, over medium-hot coals 5 to 6 minutes per side or until fish flakes when tested with fork. Transfer to plate; flake with fork.

3. Arrange salmon evenly over half of each tortilla, leaving 1-inch border. Sprinkle with cheese and jalapeño pepper slices. Fold tortillas in half. Brush tortillas with remaining 1 tablespoon oil.

4. Grill quesadillas over medium-hot coals until browned on both sides and cheese is melted. Serve with Cucumber Salsa.   *Makes 4 servings*

Lime-Poached Fish with Corn and Chili Salsa

Prep and Cook Time: 15 minutes

4 swordfish steaks,* 1-inch thick (about 1½ pounds)
1 cup baby carrots, cut lengthwise into halves
2 green onions, cut into 1-inch pieces
3 tablespoons lime juice
½ teaspoon salt, divided
½ teaspoon chili powder
1½ cups chopped tomatoes
1 cup frozen corn, thawed
1 can (4 ounces) chopped green chiles, drained
2 tablespoons chopped fresh cilantro
1 tablespoon butter or margarine

*Tuna or halibut steaks can be substituted.

1. Place fish and carrots in saucepan just large enough to hold them in single layer. Add onions, lime juice, ¼ teaspoon salt and chili powder. Add enough water to just cover fish.

2. Bring to a simmer over medium heat. Cook 8 minutes or until center of fish begins to flake when tested with fork. Transfer fish to serving plates.

3. Meanwhile, to prepare salsa, combine tomatoes, corn, chiles, cilantro and remaining ¼ teaspoon salt in medium bowl; toss well.

4. Drain carrots and onions; add butter. Transfer to serving plates; serve with salsa.   *Makes 4 servings*

*Tip

If time allows, prepare the salsa in advance so the flavors have more time to develop. Do not add salt until ready to serve. Cover and refrigerate salsa up to 1 day before serving.

Fish Tacos with Yogurt Sauce

Yogurt Sauce
- ½ **cup plain yogurt**
- ¼ **cup chopped fresh cilantro**
- 3 **tablespoons sour cream**
- **Juice of 1 lime**
- 1 **tablespoon mayonnaise**
- ½ **teaspoon ground cumin**
- ¼ **teaspoon ground red pepper**
- **Salt and black pepper**

Tacos
- **Juice of ½ lime**
- 2 **tablespoons canola oil**
- 1½ **pounds swordfish, halibut or tilapia fillets**
- **Salt and black pepper**
- 12 **corn or flour tortillas**
- 3 **cups shredded cabbage or coleslaw mix**
- 2 **medium tomatoes, chopped**

1. To prepare Yogurt Sauce, combine all sauce ingredients except salt and pepper. Season with salt and pepper to taste. Refrigerate until ready to use.

2. To prepare tacos, spray grill grid or grill basket with nonstick cooking spray. Preheat grill or broiler. Combine lime juice and oil in small bowl. About 5 minutes before cooking, brush or spoon lime mixture over fish fillets and season with salt and pepper. (Do not marinate fish longer than about 5 minutes or acid in lime will begin to "cook" fish.)

3. Grill fish over medium heat 5 minutes; turn fish and cover grill. Cook 5 minutes more; remove from grill. (If broiling fish, spray broiler pan with nonstick cooking spray. Broil 4 inches from heat about 5 minutes; turn and broil 5 minutes more or until opaque in center. Remove from broiler.) Flake fish or break into large pieces, if desired.

4. Place tortillas on grill over medium heat 10 seconds on each side or until beginning to bubble and brown lightly. Fill tortillas with fish. Top with sauce, cabbage and tomatoes. *Makes 6 servings*

Chile 'n Lime Shrimp

Prep Time: 5 minutes • **Cook Time:** 6 minutes

- ⅓ cup *Frank's® RedHot®* Chile 'n Lime™ Hot Sauce
- 2 tablespoons olive oil
- 1 teaspoon minced garlic
- 1 pound large shrimp, shelled and deveined
- 1 cup chopped green, red or yellow bell pepper
- ½ cup chopped red onion

HEAT **Chile 'n Lime™** Hot Sauce, oil and garlic in medium skillet. Cook over high heat until sauce is bubbly, stirring often.

ADD shrimp, bell pepper and onion. Cook, stirring, 3 to 5 minutes until shrimp are pink and coated with sauce. Serve with rice, if desired.

Makes 3 to 4 servings

Crab Salad with Chiles and Cilantro

- 1 cup sour cream
- 1 can (4 ounces) ORTEGA® Diced Green Chiles
- ½ cup finely chopped onion
- ¼ cup chopped fresh cilantro
- 2 tablespoons lime juice
- ½ teaspoon salt
- 1 pound fresh imitation crabmeat, chopped
  Crackers and/or tortilla chips

COMBINE sour cream, chiles, onion, cilantro, lime juice and salt in medium bowl; add crabmeat. Toss to coat well; cover. Chill for at least 1 hour.

SERVE with crackers or tortilla chips or use as a topping for salads.

Makes 4 servings

Fillets with Mole Verde

4 tablespoons vegetable oil, divided
¼ cup chopped white onion
1 or 2 fresh jalapeño peppers,* seeded and finely chopped
1 can (8 ounces) tomatillos, drained and chopped
2 cloves garlic, minced
¼ teaspoon ground cumin
⅓ cup plus 1 tablespoon water, divided
⅓ cup coarsely chopped fresh cilantro
½ teaspoon salt, divided
⅓ cup all-purpose flour
⅛ teaspoon black pepper
2 tablespoons butter or margarine
1½ to 2 pounds small red snapper or skinless sole fillets

*Jalapeño peppers can sting and irritate the skin, so wear rubber gloves when handling peppers and do not touch your eyes.

1. Heat 2 tablespoons oil in small skillet over medium heat until hot. Add onion and jalapeño peppers. Cook and stir 4 minutes or until softened. Add tomatillos, garlic and cumin. Cook and stir 1 minute.

2. Add ⅓ cup water, cilantro and ¼ teaspoon salt. Bring to a boil over high heat. Reduce heat to low. Cover and simmer 20 minutes. Pour into blender; process until smooth. Return sauce to skillet; remove from heat. Set aside.

3. Combine flour, remaining ¼ teaspoon salt and black pepper on plate.

4. Heat butter and remaining 2 tablespoons oil in 12-inch skillet over medium-high heat until foamy. Working with as many fillets as will fit in skillet in single layer, lightly coat each fillet on both sides with flour mixture; shake off excess. Cook 4 to 8 minutes until light brown on outside and opaque at center, turning once. Remove to serving plate; keep warm. Repeat with remaining fillets.

5. Quickly heat reserved sauce over medium heat until hot, stirring frequently. Pour over fish. Garnish as desired.   *Makes 4 to 6 servings*

Shrimp
Enchiladas

Prep Time: 10 minutes • **Cook Time:** 40 minutes

>   1 jar (1 pound 10 ounces) RAGÚ® Old World Style® Pasta
>   Sauce
>   1 can (4 ounces) chopped green chilies, drained
> 1½ tablespoons chili powder
>   1 pound cooked shrimp, coarsely chopped
>   2 cups shredded Monterey Jack cheese (about 8 ounces)
>   1 container (8 ounces) sour cream
>   1 package (8 ounces) corn tortillas (12 tortillas), softened

1. Preheat oven to 400°F. In medium bowl, combine Ragú Pasta Sauce, chilies and chili powder. Evenly spread 1 cup sauce mixture in 13×9-inch baking dish; set aside.

2. In another medium bowl, combine shrimp, 1 cup cheese and sour cream. Evenly spread mixture onto tortillas; roll up. Arrange seam side down in prepared dish and top with remaining sauce mixture. Cover with aluminum foil and bake 20 minutes.

3. Remove foil and sprinkle with remaining 1 cup cheese. Bake an additional 5 minutes or until cheese is melted.   *Makes 6 servings*

*Tip

To soften tortillas, arrange on a microwave-safe plate, cover with a dampened paper towel and microwave on HIGH 30 seconds.

Tortilla Soup with Grouper

1 tablespoon vegetable oil
1 small onion, chopped
2 cloves garlic, minced
3½ cups chicken broth
1½ cups tomato juice
1 cup chopped tomatoes
1 can (4 ounces) diced green chiles, drained
2 teaspoons Worcestershire sauce
1 teaspoon ground cumin
1 teaspoon chili powder
1 teaspoon salt
⅛ teaspoon black pepper
3 corn tortillas, cut into 1-inch strips
1 cup whole kernel corn
1 pound grouper fillets, washed, patted dry and cut into 1-inch cubes
Fresh parsley sprigs and jalapeño pepper* rings (optional)

*Jalapeño peppers can sting and irritate the skin, so wear rubber gloves when handling peppers and do not touch your eyes.

1. Heat oil in large saucepan over medium-high heat. Add onion and garlic and cook until softened. Stir in broth, tomato juice, tomatoes, chiles, Worcestershire, cumin, chili powder, salt and pepper. Bring to a boil; cover and simmer 10 minutes.

2. Add tortillas and corn to broth mixture; cover and simmer 8 to 10 minutes.

3. Stir in grouper. Do not cover. Continue to simmer until fish is opaque and flakes easily when tested with fork.

4. Garnish with parsley and jalapeño rings, if desired. Serve immediately.

Makes 6 servings

Shrimp and Black Bean Wraps

4 large flour tortillas
1 tablespoon olive oil
8 ounces small raw shrimp, peeled and deveined
1 (15-ounce) can black beans, drained
1 large tomato, chopped
2 green onions, sliced
1½ teaspoons TABASCO® brand Pepper Sauce
½ teaspoon salt

Preheat oven to 375°F. Wrap tortillas in foil; place in oven 10 minutes to warm. Heat oil in 10-inch skillet over medium-high heat. Add shrimp; cook and stir until pink. Mash ½ cup beans in medium bowl; stir in remaining beans, shrimp, tomato, green onions, TABASCO® Sauce and salt. To assemble, place ¼ of mixture on each tortilla; roll up tortillas, tucking in sides.   *Makes 4 servings*

*Tip

Shrimp are available raw or cooked, fresh or frozen, and unshelled or peeled. All should feel firm to the touch. Cooked shelled shrimp should be plump. Raw shrimp should not smell of ammonia.

Salmon with Cranberry-Poblano Salsa

1 poblano pepper,* finely chopped
½ cup drained pineapple tidbits
½ cup dried sweetened cranberries
¼ cup finely chopped red onion
2 tablespoons chopped fresh cilantro
1 teaspoon grated lemon peel
2 tablespoons lemon juice
4 salmon fillets (6 ounces each), skinned
Salt and black pepper

*Poblano peppers are very dark green, large triangular-shaped chiles with pointed ends. Poblanos are usually 3½ to 5 inches long. Their flavor ranges from mild to quite hot. For a milder flavor, Anaheims can be substituted.

1. Preheat broiler. Combine poblano pepper, pineapple, cranberries, onion, cilantro, lemon peel and juice in medium bowl. Toss gently and thoroughly to blend. Let stand 15 minutes to absorb flavors.

2. Spray broiler pan and rack with nonstick cooking spray. Arrange fillets on rack. Sprinkle lightly with salt and pepper. Broil 5 minutes; turn and sprinkle lightly with salt and pepper. Broil 5 minutes more or until opaque in center. Serve fillets with Cranberry-Poblano Salsa.   *Makes 4 servings*

*Tip

For extra citrus flavor, add the juice of 1 to 2 limes to salsa.

Clams
Picante

16 cherrystone clams,* scrubbed and soaked
1 can (16 ounces) whole kernel corn, drained
2 cups peeled, seeded and chopped cucumbers
1 cup chopped tomatoes
1 can (4 ounces) diced green chiles
¼ cup chopped onion
2 tablespoons lime juice
1 tablespoon chopped fresh cilantro
  Tortilla chips or soft flour tortillas (optional)

*If fresh clams in shells are not available, substitute ¾ to 1 cup shucked clams. Steam in vegetable steamer until firm. Chop clams. Omit step 1.

1. Place 1 cup water in large stockpot. Bring to a boil over high heat. Add clams. Cover and reduce heat to medium. Steam 5 to 7 minutes or until clams open. Remove clams as they open. (Discard any clams that remain unopened.) Remove clams from shells and chop.

2. Combine clams, corn, cucumbers, tomatoes, chiles, onion, lime juice and cilantro in glass bowl. Cover and refrigerate several hours or overnight to allow flavors to blend. Serve with tortilla chips, if desired.

Makes about 4 cups

na Quesadilla Stack

Prep and Cook Time: 25 minutes

4 (10-inch) flour tortillas
¼ cup plus 2 tablespoons pinto or black bean dip
1 can (9 ounces) tuna packed in water, drained and flaked
2 cups (8 ounces) shredded Cheddar cheese
1 can (14½ ounces) diced tomatoes, drained
½ cup thinly sliced green onions
1½ teaspoons butter or margarine, melted

1. Preheat oven to 400°F.

2. Place 1 tortilla on 12-inch pizza pan. Spread with 2 tablespoons bean dip, leaving ½-inch border. Top with one third each of tuna, cheese, tomatoes and green onions. Repeat layers twice, beginning with tortilla and ending with onions.

3. Top with remaining tortilla, pressing gently. Brush with melted butter.

4. Bake 15 minutes or until cheese melts and top is lightly browned. Cool. Cut into 8 wedges. *Makes 4 servings*

*Tip

For a special touch, serve with assorted toppings, such as guacamole, sour cream and salsa.

Grilled Tequila Lime Shrimp

Prep Time: 15 minutes • **Marinate Time:** 30 minutes
Cook Time: 10 minutes

1 cup LAWRY'S® Tequila Lime Marinade With Lime Juice, divided
1 pound large uncooked shrimp, peeled and deveined
8 wooden skewers, soaked in water for 15 minutes
1 yellow bell pepper, cut into 1½-inch pieces
6 green onions, sliced into 1½-inch pieces
16 cherry or pear tomatoes
1 lime, sliced into 8 wedges

In large resealable plastic bag, combine ½ cup Lawry's Tequila Lime Marinade With Lime Juice and shrimp; turn to coat. Close bag and marinate in refrigerator 30 minutes. Remove shrimp from Marinade, discarding Marinade.

On wooden skewers, alternately thread shrimp, yellow pepper, onion and tomatoes. Grill, brushing frequently with remaining ½ cup Marinade and turning once, until shrimp turn pink. Serve, if desired, with lime wedges and over hot cooked pasta, rice or orzo.   *Makes 4 servings*

Variations: Also terrific served in pita bread or flour tortilla with shredded lettuce and lime juice squeezed over the top. Both ideas are great for picnics and parties!

Tiny Seafood Tostadas

Nonstick cooking spray
**4 (8-inch) whole wheat or white flour tortillas, cut into
    32 (2½-inch) rounds or shapes**
1 cup prepared black bean dip, plus more for dipping
1 cup shredded fresh spinach
¾ cup tiny cooked or canned shrimp
¾ cup salsa
½ cup (2 ounces) shredded Monterey Jack cheese
¼ cup sour cream

1. Preheat oven to 350°F. Spray baking sheet with cooking spray. Place tortilla rounds evenly on prepared baking sheet. Lightly spray rounds with cooking spray and bake 10 minutes. Turn over and spray again; bake 3 minutes more.

2. To prepare tostadas, spread each toasted tortilla round with 1½ teaspoons black bean dip. Layer each with 1½ teaspoons shredded spinach, 1 teaspoon shrimp, 1 teaspoon salsa, sprinkle of cheese and dab of sour cream. Garnish with fresh cilantro, if desired. Serve immediately with additional bean dip.   *Makes 8 appetizer servings*

Tequila-Lime Prawns

1 pound medium raw shrimp, peeled and deveined
3 tablespoons butter or margarine
1 tablespoon olive oil
2 cloves garlic, minced
2 tablespoons tequila
1 tablespoon lime juice
¼ teaspoon salt
¼ teaspoon red pepper flakes
3 tablespoons coarsely chopped fresh cilantro
   Hot cooked rice (optional)

1. Pat shrimp dry with paper towels. Heat butter and oil in large skillet over medium heat. When butter is melted, add garlic; cook 30 seconds. Add shrimp; cook 2 minutes, stirring occasionally.

2. Add tequila, lime juice, salt and red pepper flakes. Cook 2 minutes or until most of liquid evaporates and shrimp are pink and glazed. Add cilantro; cook 10 seconds.

3. Serve over hot cooked rice, if desired. Garnish with lime wedges, if desired.   *Makes 3 to 4 servings*

*Tip

When purchasing cilantro look for bright green leaves with no signs of yellowing or wilting. To keep cilantro fresh longer, place the stem ends in a glass of water (like a bouquet), cover loosely with a plastic bag and refrigerate. Wait to wash and chop the herbs until just before using.

Spicy Fish Tacos with Fresh Salsa

Prep Time: 15 minutes • **Marinate Time :** 30 minutes
Cook Time: 5 minutes

¾ cup plus 2 tablespoons *Frank's® RedHot® Chile 'n Lime*™ Hot Sauce, divided

1 pound thick, firm white fish fillets, such as cod, halibut or sea bass, cut into ¾-inch cubes

½ cup sour cream

1½ cups finely chopped plum tomatoes

¼ cup minced fresh cilantro

2 tablespoons minced red onion

2 cups shredded iceberg lettuce

8 taco shells, warmed

1. Pour ½ cup *Chile 'n Lime*™ Hot Sauce over fish in resealable plastic bag. Marinate in refrigerator 30 minutes.

2. Combine ¼ cup *Chile 'n Lime*™ Hot Sauce and sour cream in small bowl; chill until needed.

3. Combine tomatoes, cilantro, onion and remaining 2 tablespoons *Chile 'n Lime*™ Hot Sauce. Reserve.

4. Drain fish. Heat large nonstick skillet until hot; coat with vegetable cooking spray. Stir-fry fish 3 to 5 minutes until just opaque and flakes with fork. Fill each taco shell with shredded lettuce, cooked fish and salsa. Drizzle with sour cream mixture.   *Makes 4 to 6 servings*

Variation: Substitute 1 pound peeled and deveined shrimp for fish.

Garlic Shrimp Burritos

Prep and Cook Time: 10 minutes

> 1 tablespoon vegetable oil
> 1 package (10 ounces) ready-to-use chopped romaine
>   lettuce with cabbage and carrots
> 1 teaspoon minced garlic
> 1 cup diced mango
> ½ cup sliced green onions with tops
> 8 flour tortillas (6 or 7 inches)
> 10 to 12 ounces peeled cooked medium shrimp
> ½ cup spicy black bean sauce
> ¼ teaspoon red pepper flakes
>   Salsa for garnish

1. Heat oil in large, deep skillet over medium-high heat. Add chopped romaine and garlic; stir-fry 2 minutes. Add mango and onions; stir-fry 3 minutes.

2. While vegetable mixture is cooking, stack tortillas and wrap in waxed paper. Microwave on HIGH 1½ minutes or until warm.

3. Add shrimp, spicy black bean sauce and red pepper flakes to skillet; stir-fry 2 minutes or until heated through. Spoon about ⅓ cup shrimp mixture evenly down center of each tortilla. Fold one end of tortilla over filling and roll up. Serve with salsa.   *Makes 4 servings*

Shrimp Creole
(p. 102)

Toasted Pecan-Crusted
Catfish (p. 116)

Tuna Steak with Shrimp
Creole Sauce (p. 118)

Louisiana Seafood Bake
(p. 112)

Southern **Favorites**

Blackened Catfish with Easy Tartar Sauce and Rice

Easy Tartar Sauce (recipe follows)
4 catfish fillets (4 ounces each)
2 teaspoons lemon juice
Garlic-flavored cooking spray
2 teaspoons blackened or Cajun seasoning blend
1 cup hot cooked rice

1. Prepare Easy Tartar Sauce.

2. Rinse catfish and pat dry with paper towel. Sprinkle with lemon juice; coat with cooking spray. Sprinkle with seasoning blend; coat again with cooking spray.

3. Heat large nonstick skillet over medium-high heat. Add 2 fillets to skillet seasoned side down. Cook 3 minutes per side. Reduce heat to medium and cook 3 minutes more or until fish begins to flake when tested with fork. Remove fillets from skillet; keep warm. Repeat with remaining fillets. Serve with tartar sauce and rice.   *Makes 4 servings*

Easy Tartar Sauce

¼ cup mayonnaise
2 tablespoons sweet pickle relish
1 teaspoon lemon juice

Combine mayonnaise, relish and lemon juice in small bowl; mix well. Refrigerate until ready to serve.   *Makes about ¼ cup*

Shrimp
Creole

   2 tablespoons olive oil
   1½ cups chopped green bell pepper
   1 medium onion, chopped
   ⅔ cup chopped celery
   2 cloves garlic, finely chopped
   1 cup uncooked rice
   1 can (about 14 ounces) diced tomatoes, drained and juice reserved
   1 to 2 teaspoons hot pepper sauce
   1 teaspoon dried oregano
   ¾ teaspoon salt
   ½ teaspoon dried thyme
   Black pepper
   1 pound medium raw shrimp, peeled and deveined
   1 tablespoon chopped fresh parsley (optional)

1. Preheat oven to 325°F. Heat olive oil in large skillet over medium-high heat. Add bell pepper, onion, celery and garlic; cook and stir 5 minutes or until vegetables are tender.

2. Add rice; cook and stir 5 minutes over medium heat. Add tomatoes, pepper sauce to taste, oregano, salt and thyme to skillet. Season with black pepper; stir until blended. Pour reserved tomato juice into 2-cup measuring cup. Add enough water to measure 1¾ cups liquid; add to skillet. Cook and stir 2 minutes.

3. Transfer mixture to 2½-quart casserole. Stir in shrimp. Bake, covered, 55 minutes or until rice is tender and liquid is absorbed. Garnish with parsley, if desired. *Makes 4 to 6 servings*

Louisiana Crab Dip with Crudités

1 package (8 ounces) cream cheese, softened
½ cup sour cream
3 tablespoons prepared horseradish
2 tablespoons chopped fresh parsley
1 tablespoon coarse-ground mustard
2 teaspoons TABASCO® brand Pepper Sauce
1 cup lump crabmeat, picked over and flaked
1 bag (16 ounces) baby carrots
1 bunch celery, cut into sticks
1 bunch asparagus spears, blanched
2 bunches endive
2 red or green bell peppers, cored and cut into strips

Blend cream cheese, sour cream, horseradish, parsley, mustard and TABASCO® Sauce in medium bowl until well mixed. Stir in crabmeat.

Arrange carrots, celery, asparagus, endive and peppers on large platter. Serve with dip. *Makes about 2 cups dip*

Cajun Blackened Tuna

2 tablespoons butter, melted
4 (1-inch-thick) tuna steaks (6 ounces each)
1½ teaspoons garlic salt
1 teaspoon paprika
1 teaspoon dried thyme or oregano
½ teaspoon ground cumin
¼ teaspoon ground red pepper
⅛ teaspoon white pepper
⅛ teaspoon black pepper
4 lemon wedges

1. Prepare grill or heat grill pan over medium-high heat. Brush butter over both sides of tuna. Combine remaining ingredients; mix well and sprinkle over both sides of tuna.

2. Place tuna on grid over medium-hot coals or in preheated grill pan. Grill 2 to 3 minutes per side for medium-rare tuna (do not overcook or tuna will become dry and tough). Serve with lemon wedges.

Makes 4 servings

sh Stick Po' Boys

Prep Time: 5 minutes • **Cook Time:** 13 minutes

½ cup *French's® Gourmayo™* **Wasabi Horseradish Light Mayonnaise**
¼ cup *French's®* **Spicy Brown Mustard**
¼ cup **dill pickle relish**
1 box (10.1 ounces) **fish sticks**
4 soft **hoagie rolls, split**
1 cup **shredded lettuce**
1 cup **chopped tomatoes**

1. Combine mayonnaise, mustard and relish.

2. Heat oven to 400°F. Bake fish sticks according to package directions.

3. To assemble sandwiches, spread mayonnaise mixture on cut surfaces of rolls. Arrange fish sticks on bottom half of rolls, dividing evenly. Top with lettuce and tomatoes and cover with top halves of rolls.

Makes 4 servings

*Tip

Serve mayonnaise mixture as a dip for shrimp or crab cocktail or as an accompaniment to broiled, baked, or fried seafood.

Herbed Pecan Crusted Scallops

Prep Time: 30 minutes • **Total Time:** 40 minutes

½ **cup toasted pecan pieces**
⅓ **cup fresh oregano leaves**
¼ **cup fresh thyme leaves**
3 **cloves garlic, cut up**
2 **teaspoons HERB-OX® chicken flavored bouillon**
1 **teaspoon freshly shredded lemon peel**
¼ **teaspoon ground black pepper**
3 **tablespoons olive oil**
1 **pound sea scallops (12 to 15 per pound)**

In work bowl of food processor, combine pecan pieces, herbs, garlic, bouillon, lemon peel and pepper until a paste forms. With machine running, gradually drizzle in olive oil until mixture forms a paste. Rub paste onto scallops. Thread scallops onto 4 skewers. Grill scallops over medium heat for 5 to 8 minutes or until opaque.   *Makes 4 servings*

Farm-Raised Catfish with Bacon and Horseradish

6 farm-raised catfish fillets (4 to 5 ounces each)
2 tablespoons butter
¼ cup chopped onion
1 package (8 ounces) cream cheese, softened
¼ cup dry white wine
2 tablespoons prepared horseradish
1 tablespoon Dijon mustard
½ teaspoon salt
⅛ teaspoon black pepper
4 strips bacon, cooked crisp and crumbled
2 tablespoons finely chopped fresh parsley (optional)

1. Rinse fish fillets and pat dry. Preheat oven to 350°F. Spray large baking dish with nonstick cooking spray. Arrange fillets in single layer in dish.

2. Melt butter in small skillet over medium-high heat. Add onion; cook and stir until softened. Combine cream cheese, wine, horseradish, mustard, salt and pepper in small bowl; stir in onion. Pour mixture over fish and top with crumbled bacon. Bake 30 minutes or until fish flakes easily when tested with fork. Garnish with parsley, if desired. Serve immediately. *Makes 6 servings*

Louisiana Seafood
Bake

1 can (14½ ounces) whole tomatoes, undrained and cut up
1 can (8 ounces) tomato sauce
1 cup water
1 cup sliced celery
⅔ cup uncooked regular rice
1⅓ cups *French's*® French Fried Onions, divided
1 teaspoon *Frank's*® *RedHot*® Original Cayenne Pepper Sauce
½ teaspoon garlic powder
¼ teaspoon dried oregano, crumbled
¼ teaspoon dried thyme, crumbled
½ pound white fish, thawed if frozen and cut into 1-inch chunks
1 can (4 ounces) shrimp, drained
⅓ cup sliced pitted ripe olives
¼ cup (1 ounce) grated Parmesan cheese

Preheat oven to 375°F. In 1½-quart casserole, combine tomatoes, tomato sauce, water, celery, uncooked rice, ⅔ *cup* French Fried Onions and seasonings. Bake, covered, at 375°F for 20 minutes. Stir in fish, shrimp and olives. Bake, covered, 20 minutes or until heated through. Top with cheese and remaining ⅔ *cup* onions; bake, uncovered, 3 minutes or until onions are golden brown.   *Makes 4 servings*

Microwave Directions: In 2-quart microwave-safe casserole, prepare rice mixture as above. Cook, covered, on HIGH 15 minutes, stirring rice halfway through cooking time. Add fish, shrimp and olives. Cook, covered, 12 to 14 minutes or until rice is cooked. Stir casserole halfway through cooking time. Top with cheese and remaining ⅔ *cup* onions; cook, uncovered, 1 minute. Let stand 5 minutes.

Seafood
Gumbo

½ cup chopped onion
½ cup chopped green pepper
½ cup (about 2 ounces) sliced fresh mushrooms
1 clove garlic, minced
2 tablespoons margarine
1 can (28 ounces) whole tomatoes, undrained
2 cups chicken broth
½ to ¾ teaspoon ground red pepper
½ teaspoon dried thyme leaves
½ teaspoon dried basil leaves
1 package (10 ounces) frozen cut okra, thawed
¾ pound white fish, cut into 1-inch pieces
½ pound peeled, deveined shrimp
3 cups hot cooked rice

Cook onion, green pepper, mushrooms, and garlic in margarine in large saucepan or Dutch oven over medium-high heat until tender crisp. Stir in tomatoes and juice, broth, ground red pepper, thyme, and basil. Bring to a boil. Reduce heat; simmer, uncovered, 10 to 15 minutes. Stir in okra, fish, and shrimp; simmer until fish flakes with fork, 5 to 8 minutes. Serve rice on top of gumbo.   *Makes 6 servings*

Favorite recipe from **USA Rice**

*Tip

When storing fresh fish, wrap it tightly in plastic wrap. If possible, place the package on ice and store it in the coldest part of the refrigerator. Be sure that melting ice drains away from the fish. If the flesh comes in contact with moisture, it may become discolored. Fresh fish should be used within a day.

Toasted Pecan-Crusted Catfish

8 ounces FISHER® CHEF'S NATURALS® Pecan Chips (2 cups)
2 egg whites, beaten
¼ cup milk
1 teaspoon salt
½ teaspoon black pepper
4 (6-ounce) catfish fillets, rinsed and patted dry
2 tablespoons butter, divided
2 tablespoons vegetable oil, divided

1. Place a 12-inch skillet over medium-high heat until hot. Add pecans and cook 3 minutes or until lightly browned, stirring often. Be careful not to burn. Spread in a thin layer on a sheet of foil and cool completely (about 5 minutes).

2. Place cooled pecans in a blender with salt and pepper and pulse to a fine texture. Place pecan mixture into a shallow pan (such as a pie plate).

3. Meanwhile, beat egg whites and milk in a shallow pan and until well combined.

4. Dip catfish in egg white mixture then coat evenly with pecan mixture.

5. Place the 12-inch skillet over medium-high heat until hot. Add 1 tablespoon of butter and 1 tablespoon of oil. When butter melts and begins to brown, add 2 of the fillets. Immediately reduce heat to medium and cook 4 minutes, turn and cook 4 minutes longer or until fish is opaque in center. Set aside and cover with a tent of foil to keep warm.

6. Wipe skillet with paper towel and repeat with remaining fillets.

Makes 4 servings

Tuna Steaks with Shrimp Creole Sauce

Prep Time: 15 minutes • **Cook Time:** 20 minutes

4 tablespoons olive oil, divided
1 medium red onion, chopped
1 red or yellow bell pepper, seeded and chopped
2 stalks celery, sliced
2 cloves garlic, minced
1 can (14½ ounces) stewed tomatoes
¼ cup *Frank's*® *RedHot*® Original Cayenne Pepper Sauce
¼ cup tomato paste
½ teaspoon dried thyme leaves
1 bay leaf
½ pound medium-size raw shrimp, shelled and deveined
4 tuna, swordfish or codfish steaks, cut 1 inch thick (about 1½ pounds)
Hot cooked rice (optional)

Heat 2 tablespoons oil in medium skillet over medium-high heat. Add onion, pepper, celery and garlic; cook and stir 1 minute. Stir in tomatoes, **Frank's RedHot**® Sauce, tomato paste, thyme and bay leaf. Bring to a boil. Reduce heat to medium-low. Cook 5 minutes, stirring often. Add shrimp; cook 3 minutes or until shrimp turn pink. Remove and discard bay leaf. Set aside shrimp sauce.

Brush both sides of fish steaks with remaining 2 tablespoons oil. Place steaks on grid. Grill over medium-high coals 10 minutes or until fish flakes easily with a fork,* turning once. Transfer to serving platter. Spoon shrimp sauce over fish. Serve with rice, if desired. Garnish as desired.

Makes 4 servings

*Tuna becomes dry and tough if overcooked. Cook tuna until it is opaque, but still feels somewhat soft in center. Watch carefully while grilling.

**Grilled Chinese Salmon
(p. 128)**

**Asian Shrimp & Noodle
Salad (p. 138)**

**Teriyaki Scallops
(p. 150)**

**Shrimp in Mock Lobster
Sauce (p. 126)**

Asian Fare

Orange-Glazed Salmon

Glaze
- **2 tablespoons soy sauce**
- **2 tablespoons orange juice**
- **1 tablespoon honey**
- **¾ teaspoon grated fresh ginger**
- **½ teaspoon rice wine vinegar**
- **¼ teaspoon sesame oil**

Salmon
- **4 salmon fillets (about 6 ounces each)**
- **½ teaspoon salt**
- **¼ teaspoon black pepper**
- **1 tablespoon olive oil**

1. Whisk soy sauce, juice, honey, ginger, vinegar and sesame oil in small mixing bowl; set aside.

2. Season salmon with salt and pepper. Heat olive oil in medium nonstick skillet over high heat. Arrange salmon, skin side up, in skillet. Brush with glaze. Cook salmon 4 minutes or just until center is opaque. Carefully turn; brush with glaze. Cook 4 minutes more. (Salmon will be slightly pink in the middle.)

3. Remove salmon from pan to serving plate; cover and keep warm. Place remaining glaze in small saucepan. Simmer and stir until thickened and reduced to about ¼ cup. Spoon glaze over salmon.   *Makes 4 servings*

Scallops with Vegetables

1 ounce dried mushrooms
4 teaspoons cornstarch
1 cup cold water
2½ tablespoons dry sherry
4 teaspoons soy sauce
2 teaspoons instant chicken bouillon granules
2 tablespoons vegetable oil
8 ounces fresh green beans, diagonally cut into 1-inch pieces
2 yellow onions, cut into wedges and separated
3 stalks celery, diagonally cut into ½-inch pieces
2 teaspoons minced fresh ginger
1 clove garlic, minced
1 pound fresh or thawed frozen sea scallops, cut into quarters
6 green onions, diagonally cut into thin slices
1 can (15 ounces) baby corn, drained
Whole dried mushroom and celery leaves for garnish

1. Place mushrooms in bowl; cover with hot water. Let stand 30 minutes; drain. Squeeze out as much water as possible from mushrooms. Cut off and discard stems; cut caps into thin slices.

2. Blend cornstarch and cold water in small bowl; stir in sherry, soy sauce and bouillon granules. Set aside.

3. Heat oil in wok or large skillet over high heat. Add green beans, yellow onions, celery, ginger and garlic; stir-fry 3 minutes.

4. Stir cornstarch mixture; add to wok. Cook and stir until sauce boils and thickens.

5. Add mushrooms, scallops, green onions and baby corn. Cook and stir until scallops turn opaque, about 4 minutes. Garnish, if desired.

Makes 4 to 6 servings

Shrimp in Mock Lobster Sauce

½ cup fat-free reduced-sodium beef or chicken broth
¼ cup oyster sauce
1 tablespoon cornstarch
1 egg
1 egg white
1 tablespoon peanut or canola oil
¾ pound raw medium or large shrimp, peeled and deveined
2 cloves garlic, minced
3 green onions, cut into ½-inch pieces
2 cups hot cooked Chinese egg noodles

1. Stir broth and oyster sauce into cornstarch in small bowl until smooth. Beat egg with egg white in separate small bowl. Set aside.

2. Heat wok over medium-high heat 1 minute or until hot. Drizzle oil into wok and heat 30 seconds. Add shrimp and garlic; stir-fry 3 to 5 minutes or until shrimp turn pink and opaque.

3. Stir broth mixture; add to wok. Add onions; stir-fry 1 minute or until sauce boils and thickens.

4. Stir eggs into wok; stir-fry 1 minute or just until eggs are set. Serve over noodles.   *Makes 4 servings*

Note: Oyster sauce is a thick, brown, concentrated sauce made of ground oysters, soy sauce and brine. It imparts a slight fish flavor and is used as a seasoning. It is available in the Asian section of large supermarkets.

Grilled Chinese Salmon

3 tablespoons soy sauce
2 tablespoons dry sherry
2 cloves garlic, minced
1 pound salmon fillets or steaks
Fresh cilantro

1. Combine soy sauce, sherry and garlic in shallow dish. Add salmon; turn to coat. Cover and refrigerate at least 30 minutes or up to 2 hours.

2. Drain salmon; reserve marinade. Arrange fillets skin side down on oiled rack of broiler pan or oiled grid over hot coals. Broil or grill 5 to 6 inches from heat 10 minutes. Baste with reserved marinade after 5 minutes of broiling; discard any remaining marinade. Garnish with cilantro.

Makes 4 servings

*Tip

Fish fillets and steaks should have moist flesh that is free from discoloration and skin that is shiny and resilient. If the fillet or steak has a strong odor, it is not fresh.

Jade Salad with Sesame Vinaigrette

Prep Time: 15 minutes

5 cups fresh spinach or romaine leaves, torn
1 (7-ounce) STARKIST Flavor Fresh Pouch® Tuna (Albacore or Chunk Light)
1 cup frozen cooked bay shrimp, thawed
¾ cup shredded cucumber
½ cup shredded red radishes

Sesame Vinaigrette
  3 tablespoons rice vinegar or cider vinegar
  2 tablespoons sesame oil
  2 tablespoons vegetable oil
  2 teaspoons soy sauce
  2 teaspoons sesame seeds
  1 teaspoon sugar
  Salt and pepper to taste

In a large salad bowl, toss together spinach, tuna, shrimp, cucumber and radishes. For dressing, in a shaker jar, combine vinaigrette ingredients. Cover and shake until well blended. Drizzle over salad; toss well.

Makes 4 servings

Veggie and Scallop Stir-Fry

Prep Time: 3 minutes • **Cook Time:** 10 to 12 minutes

1 tablespoon vegetable oil
1 bag (16 ounces) BIRDS EYE® frozen Pepper Stir-Fry
½ pound small sea scallops
1 small onion, chopped *or* 3 green onions, sliced
1 tablespoon light soy sauce
1 tablespoon Oriental salad dressing
⅛ teaspoon ground ginger
Garlic powder
Salt and black pepper
Hot cooked rice (optional)

• In wok or large skillet, heat oil over medium heat.

• Add vegetables; cover and cook 3 to 5 minutes or until crisp-tender.

• Uncover; add scallops and onion. Stir-fry 2 minutes.

• Stir in soy sauce and Oriental salad dressing.

• Reduce heat to low; simmer 3 to 5 minutes or until some liquid is absorbed.

• Stir in ginger, garlic powder and salt and pepper to taste; increase heat to medium-high. Stir-fry until all liquid is absorbed and scallops turn opaque and begin to brown.

• Serve over rice, if desired.   *Makes 4 servings*

Grilled Chicken & Jumbo Prawn Satay Pasta Salad

Prep Time: 15 minutes • **Cook Time:** 5 minutes

1 pound boneless chicken, cut into 1-inch cubes
1 pound jumbo shrimp, peeled and deveined
¼ cup *Frank's® RedHot®* Buffalo Wing Sauce
⅓ cup chunky peanut butter
¼ cup orange juice
2 tablespoons reduced-sodium teriyaki sauce
1 tablespoon minced fresh cilantro
2 teaspoons finely minced fresh ginger
4 cups cooked linguine (about 8 ounces uncooked)

1. Thread chicken and shrimp on separate metal skewers; set aside. Combine Wing Sauce, peanut butter, orange juice, teriyaki sauce, cilantro and ginger. Pour ¾ cup into small bowl and reserve.

2. Grill chicken and shrimp about 5 minutes until cooked, basting with remaining Wing Sauce mixture.

3. Place pasta in large bowl. Toss with reserved Wing Sauce mixture. Arrange chicken and shrimp on top. Serve immediately. If desired, garnish with peanuts, red bell peppers, cucumber, green onion and chopped cilantro.   *Makes 6 to 8 servings*

*Tip
If sauce becomes too thick, thin with additional orange juice.

Szechuan Tuna
Steaks

4 tuna steaks (6 ounces each), cut 1 inch thick
¼ cup dry sherry or sake
¼ cup soy sauce
1 tablespoon dark sesame oil
1 teaspoon hot chili oil *or* ¼ teaspoon red pepper flakes
1 clove garlic, minced
3 tablespoons chopped fresh cilantro

1. Place tuna in single layer in large shallow glass dish. Combine sherry, soy sauce, sesame oil, hot chili oil and garlic in small bowl. Reserve ¼ cup soy sauce mixture at room temperature. Pour remaining soy sauce mixture over tuna. Cover; marinate in refrigerator 40 minutes, turning once.

2. Spray grid with nonstick cooking spray. Prepare grill for direct grilling.

3. Drain tuna, discarding marinade. Place tuna on grid. Grill, uncovered, over medium-hot coals 6 minutes or until tuna is opaque, but still feels somewhat soft in center,* turning halfway through grilling time. Transfer tuna to carving board. Cut each tuna steak into thin slices; fan out slices onto serving plates. Drizzle tuna slices with reserved soy sauce mixture; sprinkle with cilantro.   *Makes 4 servings*

*Tuna becomes dry and tough if overcooked. Cook it as if it were beef.

Oriental Baked Cod

2 tablespoons reduced-sodium soy sauce
2 tablespoons apple juice
1 tablespoon finely chopped fresh ginger
2 cloves garlic, minced
1 teaspoon crushed Szechuan peppercorns
4 cod fillets (about 1 pound)
4 green onions, thinly sliced

1. Preheat oven to 375°F. Spray roasting pan with nonstick cooking spray; set aside.

2. Combine soy sauce, apple juice, ginger, garlic and peppercorns in small bowl; mix well.

3. Place cod fillets in prepared pan; pour soy sauce mixture over fish. Bake about 10 minutes or until fish is opaque and flakes easily when tested with fork.

4. Transfer cod to serving dish; pour pan juices over fish and sprinkle with green onions. Garnish, if desired.   *Makes 4 servings*

Asian Shrimp & Noodle Salad

Prep Time: 15 minutes • **Cook Time:** 10 minutes

- ⅓ **cup plus 2 tablespoons vegetable oil, divided**
- ¼ **cup cider vinegar**
- **2 tablespoons** *French's®* **Worcestershire Sauce**
- **2 tablespoons light soy sauce**
- **2 tablespoons honey**
- **1 teaspoon grated fresh ginger** *or* ¼ **teaspoon ground ginger**
- **2 packages (3 ounces each) chicken-flavor ramen noodle soup**
- **1 pound raw shrimp, peeled and deveined with tails left on**
- **2 cups vegetables such as broccoli, carrots and snow peas, cut into bite-size pieces**
- **1**⅓ **cups** *French's®* **French Fried Onions, divided**

1. Combine ⅓ cup oil, vinegar, Worcestershire, soy sauce, honey and ginger until well blended; set aside. Prepare ramen noodles according to package directions for soup; drain and rinse noodles. Place in large serving bowl.

2. Stir-fry shrimp in 1 tablespoon oil in large skillet over medium-high heat, stirring constantly, until shrimp turn pink. Remove shrimp to bowl with noodles. Stir-fry vegetables in remaining oil in skillet over medium-high heat, stirring constantly, until vegetables are crisp-tender.

3. Add vegetable mixture, dressing and *1 cup* French Fried Onions to bowl with noodles; toss to coat well. Serve immediately topped with remaining onions.

Makes 6 servings

*Tip

Purchase cut-up vegetables from the salad bar of your local supermarket to save prep time.

Wasabi
Salmon

2 tablespoons soy sauce
1½ teaspoons wasabi paste or wasabi prepared from powder,
   divided, plus more to taste
4 salmon fillets (6 ounces each)
¼ cup mayonnaise

1. Prepare grill or preheat broiler. Combine soy sauce and ½ teaspoon wasabi paste; mix well. Spoon mixture over salmon. Place salmon on grid over medium coals or on rack of broiler pan. Grill or broil 4 to 5 inches from heat source 8 minutes or until salmon is opaque in center.

2. Meanwhile, combine mayonnaise and remaining 1 teaspoon wasabi paste; mix well. Taste and add more wasabi, if desired. Transfer salmon to serving plates; top with mayonnaise mixture.   *Makes 4 servings*

*Tip

Wasabi is sometimes referred to as Japanese horseradish. It has a fiery flavor.

Spicy Shrimp with Snow Peas

Prep Time: 35 minutes

6 ounces fresh snow peas, trimmed
1 medium red bell pepper, cut in ½-inch strips
½ cup diagonally sliced green onions
1 tablespoon MAZOLA® Oil
1 cup Orient Express Stir-Fry Sauce (recipe follows)
1 teaspoon crushed red pepper
1 pound medium raw shrimp, peeled and deveined
Rice (optional)

Microwave Directions

1. In 3-quart microwavable casserole combine snow peas, bell pepper, green onions and oil. Microwave covered on HIGH (100%) 1 minute.

2. Stir in Stir-Fry Sauce and crushed red pepper. Microwave 2 minutes. Add shrimp. Microwave 6 to 8 minutes or until sauce boils and thickens and shrimp are opaque, stirring twice. If desired, serve with rice.

Makes 4 servings

Orient Express Stir-Fry Sauce

2½ cups chicken broth
½ cup ARGO® or KINGSFORD'S® Corn Starch
½ cup soy sauce
½ cup KARO® Light Corn Syrup
½ cup dry sherry
¼ cup cider vinegar
2 cloves garlic, minced or pressed
2 teaspoons grated fresh ginger
¼ teaspoon ground red pepper

1. Combine chicken broth, corn starch, soy sauce, corn syrup, sherry, vinegar, garlic, ginger and red pepper in 1½-quart jar with tight-fitting lid. Shake well.

2. Store in refrigerator up to 3 weeks. Shake well before using.

Makes about 4 cups

Curry Coconut Fried Rice

Prep Time: 25 minutes • **Cook Time:** 20 minutes

1 cup chopped red onion
2 tablespoons vegetable oil
¾ pound medium raw shrimp, peeled and deveined
¼ cup chicken broth
1 tablespoon curry powder
4 cups cooked long-grain rice
2 cups frozen mixed carrots and peas, thawed
1 tablespoon soy sauce
3 medium, firm DOLE® Bananas, sliced
½ cup flaked coconut, toasted

• Cook and stir onion in hot oil in large skillet over medium-high heat until crisp-tender.

• Add shrimp, chicken broth and curry powder; cook and stir until shrimp turn pink. Add rice, carrots and peas; cook and stir 3 to 5 minutes or until heated through.

• Stir in soy sauce. Add bananas; cook and stir 1 minute or until heated through. Sprinkle with coconut before serving. *Makes 6 servings*

Bangkok Rice and Shrimp Salad

½ **cup canned coconut milk**
¼ **cup rice vinegar**
1 **tablespoon oil**
½ **teaspoon salt**
3 **tablespoons chopped fresh basil, plus additional basil leaves for garnish**
3 **cups cooked U.S. jasmine or medium grain rice**
1 **pound frozen cooked shrimp, peeled, deveined, thawed**
½ **cup chopped salted peanuts**

Whisk coconut milk, vinegar and oil together in a small bowl. Add salt and basil. Stir rice, shrimp and coconut milk mixture in medium bowl until blended. Spoon into serving bowl; sprinkle with peanuts and basil to garnish.

Makes 6 servings

Favorite recipe from **USA Rice**

*Tip

Thai cooks rinse their rice before cooking. This isn't because it's unsanitary, but it's to rinse off some of the powder that makes cooked rice stickier and starchier. To rinse rice, place it in a bowl or saucepan, cover it with cool water and swish it around with your hand until the water becomes cloudy. Pour the water out and repeat the procedure twice more.

Chinese Crab & Cucumber Salad

1 large cucumber, peeled
12 ounces crabmeat (fresh, pasteurized or thawed frozen), picked over and flaked
½ red bell pepper, diced
½ cup mayonnaise
3 tablespoons soy sauce
1 tablespoon sesame oil
1 teaspoon ground ginger
½ pound bean sprouts
1 tablespoon sesame seeds, toasted
Fresh chives, cut into 1-inch pieces

1. Cut cucumber in half lengthwise; scoop out seeds. Cut into 1-inch pieces. Combine cucumber, crabmeat and bell pepper in large bowl.

2. Blend mayonnaise, soy sauce, sesame oil and ginger in small bowl. Pour over crabmeat mixture; toss to mix well. Refrigerate 1 hour to allow flavors to blend.

3. To serve, arrange bean sprouts on individual serving plates. Spoon crabmeat mixture on top; sprinkle with sesame seeds and chives.

Makes 4 main-dish servings

Chilled Shrimp in Chinese Mustard Sauce

1 cup water
½ cup dry white wine
2 tablespoons reduced-sodium soy sauce
½ teaspoon Szechuan or black peppercorns
1 pound large raw shrimp, peeled and deveined
¼ cup prepared sweet and sour sauce
2 teaspoons hot Chinese mustard

1. Combine water, wine, soy sauce and peppercorns in medium saucepan. Bring to a boil over high heat. Add shrimp; reduce heat to medium. Cover and simmer 2 to 3 minutes or until shrimp are opaque and cooked through. Drain well. Cover and refrigerate until chilled.

2. For mustard sauce, combine sweet and sour sauce and mustard in small bowl; mix well. Serve with shrimp. *Makes 6 servings*

Substitution: If you are unable to find hot Chinese mustard or simply want a sauce with less heat, substitute a spicy brown or Dijon mustard.

*Tip
For this quick and easy recipe, the shrimp can be prepared up to one day in advance.

Teriyaki Scallops

2 tablespoons soy sauce
1 tablespoon mirin* or sweet cooking rice wine
2 teaspoons sake or dry sherry
1 teaspoon sugar
1 pound large scallops
¼ teaspoon salt
8 ounces asparagus, diagonally sliced into 2-inch lengths
1 tablespoon vegetable oil

*Mirin is a Japanese sweet wine available in Japanese markets and the ethnic section of large supermarkets.

1. Combine soy sauce, mirin, sake and sugar in medium bowl; stir until sugar is dissolved. Add scallops; let stand 10 minutes, turning occasionally.

2. Meanwhile, bring 2½ cups water and salt to a boil in medium saucepan over high heat. Add asparagus; reduce heat to medium-high. Cook 3 to 5 minutes or until crisp-tender. Drain asparagus; keep warm.

3. Drain scallops, reserving marinade.

4. Preheat broiler. Line broiler pan with foil; brush broiler rack with vegetable oil. Place scallops on rack; brush lightly with marinade. Broil about 4 inches from heat source 4 to 5 minutes or until brown. Turn scallops with tongs; brush lightly with marinade. Broil 4 to 5 minutes or just until scallops are opaque in center. Serve immediately with asparagus.

Makes 4 servings

Vegetable-Shrimp Stir-Fry

1 tablespoon olive oil
6 ounces snow peas, trimmed
6 green onions, cut into 1-inch pieces
1 red bell pepper, cut into ½-inch strips
1 pound medium raw shrimp, peeled and deveined
¼ pound large mushrooms, quartered
2 tablespoons soy sauce
1 tablespoon seasoned rice vinegar
1 teaspoon sesame oil

1. Heat oil in large skillet or wok over medium-high heat. Add snow peas, green onions and bell pepper; stir-fry 2 minutes.

2. Add shrimp; stir-fry 2 minutes or until shrimp turn pink.

3. Add mushrooms; stir-fry until tender and most of liquid evaporates.

4. Add remaining ingredients; heat through, stirring constantly.

Makes 4 servings

*Tip

Serve this tasty stir-fry with hot cooked rice or noodles.

The publisher would like to thank the companies and organizations listed below for the use of their recipes and photographs in this publication.

ACH Food Companies, Inc.

Birds Eye Foods

Del Monte Corporation

Dole Food Company, Inc.

Filippo Berio® Olive Oil

Fisher® Nuts

Hormel Foods, LLC

McIlhenny Company (TABASCO® brand Pepper Sauce)

Mushroom Council

National Fisheries Institute

Ortega®, A Division of B&G Foods, Inc.

Reckitt Benckiser Inc.

StarKist Seafood Company

Stonyfield Farm®

Reprinted with permission of Sunkist Growers, Inc. All Rights Reserved.

Unilever

US Dry Bean Council

USA Rice FederationTM

VOLUME MEASUREMENTS (dry)

$1/8$ teaspoon = 0.5 mL
$1/4$ teaspoon = 1 mL
$1/2$ teaspoon = 2 mL
$3/4$ teaspoon = 4 mL
1 teaspoon = 5 mL
1 tablespoon = 15 mL
2 tablespoons = 30 mL
$1/4$ cup = 60 mL
$1/3$ cup = 75 mL
$1/2$ cup = 125 mL
$2/3$ cup = 150 mL
$3/4$ cup = 175 mL
1 cup = 250 mL
2 cups = 1 pint = 500 mL
3 cups = 750 mL
4 cups = 1 quart = 1 L

VOLUME MEASUREMENTS (fluid)

1 fluid ounce (2 tablespoons) = 30 mL
4 fluid ounces ($1/2$ cup) = 125 mL
8 fluid ounces (1 cup) = 250 mL
12 fluid ounces ($1 1/2$ cups) = 375 mL
16 fluid ounces (2 cups) = 500 mL

WEIGHTS (mass)

$1/2$ ounce = 15 g
1 ounce = 30 g
3 ounces = 90 g
4 ounces = 120 g
8 ounces = 225 g
10 ounces = 285 g
12 ounces = 360 g
16 ounces = 1 pound = 450 g

DIMENSIONS

$1/16$ inch = 2 mm
$1/8$ inch = 3 mm
$1/4$ inch = 6 mm
$1/2$ inch = 1.5 cm
$3/4$ inch = 2 cm
1 inch = 2.5 cm

OVEN TEMPERATURES

250°F = 120°C
275°F = 140°C
300°F = 150°C
325°F = 160°C
350°F = 180°C
375°F = 190°C
400°F = 200°C
425°F = 220°C
450°F = 230°C

BAKING PAN SIZES

Utensil	Size in Inches/Quarts	Metric Volume	Size in Centimeters
Baking or Cake Pan (square or rectangular)	$8 \times 8 \times 2$	2 L	$20 \times 20 \times 5$
	$9 \times 9 \times 2$	2.5 L	$23 \times 23 \times 5$
	$12 \times 8 \times 2$	3 L	$30 \times 20 \times 5$
	$13 \times 9 \times 2$	3.5 L	$33 \times 23 \times 5$
Loaf Pan	$8 \times 4 \times 3$	1.5 L	$20 \times 10 \times 7$
	$9 \times 5 \times 3$	2 L	$23 \times 13 \times 7$
Round Layer Cake Pan	$8 \times 1 1/2$	1.2 L	20×4
	$9 \times 1 1/2$	1.5 L	23×4
Pie Plate	$8 \times 1 1/4$	750 mL	20×3
	$9 \times 1 1/4$	1 L	23×3
Baking Dish or Casserole	1 quart	1 L	—
	$1 1/2$ quart	1.5 L	—
	2 quart	2 L	—